MW01047705

1

Touched by the Miracle

WHAT READERS SAY ABOUT THIS BOOK

Good-bye Mitch, serves as testimony to the author's faith and love. Even the casual reader will be touched by this family's loss and the strength of this mother's devotion to God. This tale is at once both heartbreaking and inspirational. The invaluable lesson contained herein is that life's most daunting challenges can yield its greatest gifts. It should be shared with all those seeking comfort during difficult times.

Mark A. Cohn
Chairman, Board of Directors, 2001-2003
Children's Hospitals and Clinics
Minneapolis/St. Paul, Minnesota

"Good-bye, Mitch"

"Good-bye, Mitch"
Sorrow, Grief, Inspiration
• •

by Rebecca Chepokas
& Ronald Stanchfield

a daughter-father collaboration

AMBER
WOODS
PUBLISHING

Amber Woods Publishing
Woodland, Minnesota

ISBN   0-9743717-4-2

Editing, Tim Remington
First Printing, Bang Printing, Brainerd, Minnesota

Amber Woods Publishing
P.O. Box 280
Excelsior, MN 55331

Contents

PART III

Dedication

This book is dedicated to people everywhere grieving the death of a loved one and to those who come alongside to comfort.

It is our prayer that all who may read this book will be comforted to the full measure with which we have been comforted.

The Chepokas Family

Acknowledgement

Words alone cannot express the depth of appreciation shared by Mitchell's family for the contributions of the countless individuals who have given their time, money, encouragement, knowledge, resources and most of all, themselves, to make Mitchell's life on earth pleasant and meaningful. For certainly without these angels and saints this book would not have come into being.

To the doctors, nurses, medical staff and technicians who stood by his side hours on end; to restaurant wait-staff, shop-keepers, teachers, friends, family and the thousands of unnamed prayer warriors from around the world who monitored Mitchell's condition daily on the Internet; to those whose efforts may have gone unnoticed, but whose value is eternal and well noted in the Lamb's Book of Life, we thank each and every one of you. And we praise our loving God that He appointed you to impact our lives at such a time as this.

Those Mitchell left behind

PREFACE

In every life there comes a season for grieving. Loss of a loved one is an expectation all peoples share, acknowledged or not. These are seasons filled with dread and gloom and emotional exhaustion.

Such seasons invade our lives like unwanted storms. Many appear far on the horizon and give us time to prepare. Some even pass over quickly and we find our preparation has sustained us. Then, despite heart-breaking loss, we are quickly able to resume our lives.

But there are those storms which come unexpectedly, without warning—those storms of which we have said, "It will never happen to me." We are caught unaware and unprepared, blind-sided.

These storms wreak havoc with our lives and, but for the grace of God, they have the ability to destroy all that we hold dear. They litter our lives with wreckage and debris, draining our lives of all goodness. When these storms pass, we can only wonder where to begin the cleanup. And we wonder are we even up to the task?

Mitchell's storm came fast and with great fury. Early clouds of Marfans Syndrome quickly mutated, assailing the Chepokas family with the unbelievable, that—"C" word—cancer! From the outset his condition was terminal.

Mitchell was a typical little boy. Aside from physical problems, which doctors attributed to his Marfans, he was normal. But unlike other boys, he was destined to endure a season of pain and disappointment beyond comprehension.

Mitchell was courageous beyond words. Family members cannot recall ever hearing him complain about the hand dealt him in life. It was a hand he played with gusto to the very last card. His heroic story warrants a book of its own in the future.

This is not a book about Mitchell Chepokas, although you will be introduced to this remarkable boy. It is a journal of his mother's passage from sorrow and grief to inspiration, it is a brief chronicle of those most touched by his life and how they are rebuilding their lives following his death.

Just as Mitchell's spirit inspired all who heard his

story, so did the faith of his father Steve, his mother Becky and his sister, Melissa. Their sustaining faith in the wake of Mitchell's death can be a source of comfort and hope for those standing vigil over the storm clouds growing on their own horizons. This is the miracle of Mitch.

Mitchie Boy

Many months have passed since my father and I began writing this book. Only now am I able to reflect with some objectivity—without tearful breakdowns—on my son's life and those qualities that gave his life special meaning. As you join me on my journey, let me introduce you to the boy that blessed our lives for a wonderful and adventure-filled nine-and-one-half years.

Over the course of his short life, Mitch embodied many good qualities we all wish to attain. He overflowed with life. He was sweet and gentle, considerate and loving and full of hope—abounding, never-ending hope. He sought to discover the wonders of life, expecting only good things to happen each day. We called him our Mitchie Boy.

Mitch was born July 30, 1993, our second gift from God. He joined his three-and-one-half-year-old sister, Melissa, and our family was complete. He slept well, ate well, was always pleasant and happy, and loved to cuddle. Mitch seemed in every way to be a healthy baby boy.

The first of many disappointing doctor appointments occurred when Mitch was 19 months old. Doctors informed us he had a concave sternum. Uncertain what that really meant, we prayed a prayer that would become so very familiar, "Lord, this precious boy was Yours before You gifted him to us. You know his every need before we do. Please guide us to know what to do for our Mitch."

A specialist confirmed that Mitch had Pectusexcvatem; his sternum was applying pressure to his heart, lungs and other internal organs. Corrective surgery was necessary, but it could wait until he turned three. The time for the surgery arrived, Mitchell understood its importance. Only slightly nervous, he underwent corrective surgery in November of 1996.

Mitchell spent the next five weeks in a half-body brace, attached by a little bungee cord that wrapped around his sternum to pull it into proper position. His goofy, self-assured personality quickly adjusted to his new appendage. When anyone asked, "Mitch, what's under your shirt?" he would smile and give them a peek.

The surgery was successful and Mitch developed like a typical boy. He loved to play, wrestle, cuddle and tease his big sister. His smile and laugh were contagious. He loved wearing his yellow puddle-jumper boots as he zoomed around on his little yellow horse-on-wheels. With the twinkle in his eye, he caused everyone to wonder, "What next"?

Soon we began to question his eyesight. At age four he failed his pre-school eye screening. We went to a pediatric eye specialist and were informed Mitchell had a severe astigmatism. From that day forward Mitch wore glasses, and he did so with pride. He was so cute! He obviously enjoyed his improved vision and excitedly took to playing T-ball, shooting hoops and riding his bike.

Shortly before he turned five, Mitchell began to experience headaches when he exerted himself or became over heated. His symptoms indicated migraines. In January of 2000, searching for the cause, doctors prescribed an MRI of his brain. They found nothing. Mitch, now six years old, moderated his activity, rested when needed, and continued on in characteristic style.

The following spring, as Mitchell was completing kindergarten, he became aware of a quick, stabbing pain in his chest that took his breath away. It occurred only a few times over several months, but it scared him. Unsure what to do and very concerned, we again prayed our familiar prayer for God's guidance.

My spirit became very restless during this period of time; I sensed something was terribly wrong with Mitch. I knew only God could remove the fear that consumed me. I prayed, "Lord, please take my fear regarding Mitch...."

Now, as I reflect back, I believe God allowed my restless spirit to prepare me for the troubled days to come. He knew I would turn to Him for strength and peace, and as I did He strengthened my faith.

In late February, 2001, I received a chilling phone call from a friend. She told me about a news report she had heard, adding, "...this sounds like Mitch!" I immediately went to my computer and searched for The National Marfans Foundation's web site, frozen with shock as I read. *Could this be Mitch's condition?* I wondered. Does he have Marfan Syndrome? Again we prayed for God's guidance.

It took a month of trips to clinics and doctors' offices to confirm that Mitchell did indeed have Marfan Syndrome, a genetic connective tissue disorder. Strangely, after undergoing a family screening, we discovered Mitch did not inherit Marfans from either Steve or me. Rather, Mitchell was the victim of *spontaneous mutation*.

At last we could understand Mitchell's changing features; tall and thin, long limbs, extremely flexible, narrow jaw, high palette and poor vision. We learned he had an enlarged aorta, a sticky heart valve, and detached lenses in his eyes. We were told he could expect other complications throughout his life.

This life-changing diagnosis seemed to be more than we could bear. It meant an end to Mitch's dreams of playing baseball or basketball or any other contact sports or high-aerobic activity. He would begin blood pressure medication to keep his heart rate down, literally, to keep his aorta from rupturing. This condition is known as *aortic dissection*, the leading cause of death among Marfan victims.

During the drive home following his diagnosis, Mitch remained quiet—very quiet—not wanting to talk. It was

25

as though he was struggling to understand, *why?* Finally he turned to me and asked, "Did Jesus want me made like this?"

Wow! I had just been praying, asking God for the words to help Mitch understand. Here was my lead-in. As God answered my prayer, I told Mitch, "Jesus would like all of us to be born with perfect bodies, but we live in a world that isn't perfect... We have to believe that Jesus has a plan for our lives, even when He allows us to become sick or have something wrong with us. Mitch, I believe Jesus has a plan for your life, and I think people will get to know Jesus because of you. I don't know how, but they will. And someday in Heaven we will all have the perfect bodies Jesus wants us to have." I couldn't have known how prophetic my words would become.

Again, Mitch adjusted incredibly well. He discovered a new sport, golf. At age seven, he decided there were many things to do in life. Mitch now wanted to be a chef or baker, a singer, guitar player or a drummer in a Christian rock band and, yes, a professional golfer. He was moving on with life.

During that winter and spring Mitch grew several

inches. He experienced a lack of energy and was often extremely tired. His joints ached, his stomach was frequently upset, symptoms we assumed of Marfans. Mitchell was becoming frustrated. Often he would say, "Do I have to go to school today? I'm tired!" But, amazingly, he still had that twinkle in his eye and a quirky sense of humor as he sought to live on the lighter, more amusing side of life.

One evening Mitch yelled from the bathroom in a sickly voice, "Mom, I need you!" I found him lying on the rug in the middle of the floor. Next to him was a small wet pile of vomit. Moaning, with sweat running down his forehead, he said, "Mom, I'm sick." As I bent down to help him, a little smirk appeared on his face. Then, suddenly he scooped up the vomit and sent it flying in my direction. I screamed, jumped and fell backward. Mitch laughed at me; pointing to the rubberized, joke piece of vomit laying in my lap. "Ha, ha, ha," squealed Mitch the jokester, always playing a trick on the unsuspecting.

On April 26, 2002, Mitchell participated in his second grade choir concert, smiling and singing joyfully as he moved about the risers to the actions of the song. He accidentally stepped off the second tier, falling to the ground and hitting his right tibia just below the knee. Holding back tears, he got up, smiled, and timidly rejoined his classmates.

The two weeks following, the limp Mitch developed grew worse and the bump on his leg grew larger. The doctor-on-call at our local clinic thought the bump to be larger than what would be expected from Mitch's fall. The x-rays showed no cracks or tears, but the bone growth was strangely fogged and spotted, like a leopard. So, concerned of possible early arthritis, he suggested that we see an orthopedic specialist. Mitchell's yearly orthopedic appointment, to evaluate his Marfans, was already scheduled for May 29, less then two weeks away.

The morning of May 29, I awoke early, feeling oddly nervous about the day to come. I found myself crying and calling out to God, "Lord, I know Mitch is in Your hands, but I don't understand what I'm feeling. I ask that You give wisdom to Mitchell's doctors today. Please let them see what You want them to see!"

That afternoon I told the doctor about Mitch's ailments. At first he was not concerned. But, after examining the large bump on his leg and after noticing a decrease in joint flexibility, he ordered full-body x-rays. Obediently Mitch struck various positions before the machine's lens. New x-ray images in hand, the doctor looked me right in the eye and asked, "How has Mitch been feeling?" I was surprised by the concern in his voice—it suggested something entirely different than Marfans. He was alarmed.

Mitch had not been feeling well. He seemed weaker and had not been eating as much. He could no longer ride his bike and was unable to run or even walk long distances. He'd take the stairs one step at a time, holding tightly to the railing. During a recent trip to Disney World, we had rented a wheel chair for him because it hurt him to walk. We believed his Marfans was worsening.

I explained to the doctor our observations of Mitch's condition over the past few months. Mitch sat behind us on the examination bed, quietly watching and listening as the doctor placed his new x-rays beside a set taken ten months earlier. "We're dealing with something other than Marfans here," the doctor said at last, a question sounding in his voice.

I looked at the x-rays. The difference was obvious. I could see the bones were cloudy, poorly defined and spotted, and the joints appeared bright white. The earlier x-rays had no discoloration. We both stood there perplexed. The doctor said, "Possibly it's something in his blood. Whatever it is, it's making Mitchell's bones sick."

We moved to a waiting room where Mitch quietly played video games. We waited for the lab to call us in for the doctor ordered blood work. Watching Mitchell, my emotions churned. The doctor's reaction concerned me. He had told Mitch to be very careful when he walked, his bones were sick and probably very weak. He instructed us to forego Mitchell's final six days of school. There would be no more school for Mitch.

Silently I prayed, "Lord, is this it? Is this why I have had such a heavy heart? Please Lord," I ask again, "let the doctors see what it is You want them to see!"

I telephoned Steve, struggling for words, able only to cry. Mitch noticed my tears after I hung up the phone. "Mom, why are you crying?" he asked lovingly. With great tenderness he said, "It'll be okay!" I could only pray our familiar prayer for God's guidance.

Over the next several days Mitch underwent numerous tests and scans. We met with an oncologist team from Fairview University Medical Center, and a bone biopsy was scheduled for June 5, 2002. On June 6, seven weeks before Mitchell's ninth birthday, we received their diagnosis; Mitchell had Osteogenic Sarcoma or Osteosarcoma—bone cancer.

Unlike the familiar form of Osteosarcoma, which is found in new growing bones and normally in only one or two locations of the body, Mitch's bones were saturated. He had cancer from head to toe, a form rarely seen, according to doctors. Furthermore, a small amount of the cancer was already in one lung, the first soft tissue organ this type of cancer will attack. Without treatment he may have only weeks to live. Mitch was in need of a miracle!

The unknown outcome of this monster—cancer—was extremely frightening. At first, Mitchell was very afraid. When he would quietly play, adjusting to a new routine, we'd ask how he was doing. He'd respond, "I don't want to talk about it!" But soon, in spite of the disheartening news, Mitchell's spirit rallied. He developed a matter-of-fact attitude and began to ask questions, determined to understand and to fight the battle he knew lay ahead.

Mitch began chemotherapy on June 11, 2002.

For the remainder of Mitchell's life he tried to focus on everything that was beneficial. He was determined not to miss any fun and he lived each day to the fullest. Most important to his family and, especially to him, Mitch believed in Jesus. And he believed in miracles. His faith was magnetic. He was unassuming and people were strangely drawn to him. Wherever he went and in everyone he encountered, he caused faces to smile, changing the lives of those whose path he crossed.

During this final time with my Mitchie Boy, a spiritual excitement filled my soul, even overpowering my fear of his approaching death. I thought of my earlier conversation with him when he asked, "Did Jesus want me made like this?" Miraculously, the words God had given me on that day came to fruition. Mitchell's life reflected the love and power of the sovereign God and creator of the universe. People saw Jesus in our Mitchie Boy!

Introduction

This journey begins as Mitchell enters the last three weeks of his life on earth. For the purpose of this book we have included the story, "Mitchell's Voyage Home," which appeared in local newspapers in Minneapolis, and Anna Maria, Florida, following Mitchell's death.

Mitchell's Grandfather and co-author of "Good-bye Mitch" wrote the original text for the article. We reprint segments of it here, interspersed with my personal reflections written as the incidents they portray occur, from when the *voyage* began to today—one year after Mitchell's death.

Readers can easily follow this final period in Mitchell's life, his death and beyond, as it unfolds in his grandfather's narratives, and the short chapters that follow in which I describe my difficult journey.

Mitchell's Voyage Home

(Excerpt from *Mitchell's Voyage Home*, by Ronald Stanchfield)

Like a few granules of salt in a jar of black pepper, their white "T" shirts seemed to be everywhere. They numbered only thirty five, yet they stood out in the crowd of 3,300 passengers on board the cruise ship, "Adventures of the Sea" cruising toward destinations in the Southern Caribbean.

Each "T" shirt bore the inscription, "It's All About Mitch," a statement of the group's purpose and their motivation for making the journey. It also identified Mitchell's website, www.miraclesformitch.com, a name reflecting the group's prayers and aspirations for Mitch's healing.

These were the parents, family, and friends of Mitchell Chepokas who, at age nine, was entering the last days of his life. Indeed, it was miraculous he had made it this far; that he had lived with the disease this long, as cancer ate away at his bones. This adventure would be the last before Mitchell's final journey, to "his new home in

Heaven."

It was April, 2001, when Mitchell learned he was a victim of the genetic disorder, Marfans Syndrome, that would dramatically alter his life. Then on June 6, 2002, he learned he had cancer, which would take his life.

During the months of treatment that followed, Mitchell focused on life's positives and pursued dreams shared by his parents, Steve and Becky, and his sister, Melissa. Despite increasing pain and decreasing mobility he refused to complain. He became a hometown celebrity, rallying support and inspiring thousands as a champion for Children's Cancer Research Fund.

He was a frequent guest on local radio talk shows and the subject of numerous newspaper articles. Mitchell, along with family, became an inspiration for thousands of strangers from throughout the world who visited his website daily.

Still he dreamed of a grand adventure he could share with his family, his grandparents and close friends, all of them traveling together on a cruise. The dates were set and reservations made. It was a goal he'd live for.

On the eve of their departure, because of his

weakened state, Mitchell's parents gave him one last chance to call off the trip. He refused. So, early the next morning, the group joined the thousands departing the Twin Cities airport for spring break destinations. When Mitchell and his family left their Chanhassen home on the morning of March 23, he left home forever.

Because of limited seating the group took two different fights to San Juan, Puerto Rico, their port of embarkation. Heightened security caused by the war with Iraq made navigating security and check points arduous and painful for Mitchell as his mother maneuvered his wheel chair slowly through long, serpentine lines.

The first leg of their journey was in cramped coach-class seating. Then, during a plane change in Memphis, prayers were answered when several first class passengers, who had been made aware of Mitchell's condition by Northwest Airlines personnel, gave up their seats. Miraculously, Mitchell and his entourage of nine would complete the second leg of their journey together and in comfort.

In San Juan, cruise line personnel quickly ushered Mitch, mom, dad, and sister onto a bus, bypassing further waiting, and delivered him shipside. Moments later he lay on his stateroom bed looking out an open balcony to the sea. But he had paid a price for this first leg of their adventure—increased pain, muscle spasms, and unimaginable discomfort.

Their cabin steward's name was Sean. Becky and Steve Chepokas believe he was "their angel." The young man shared the Chepokas family's evangelistic Christian beliefs and was a member of an onboard congregation made up of ship's personnel.

By the time Mitch's grandparents had located their room next door, Sean arrived with the ship's pastor for a time of prayer. The Pastor prayed for the family's well being, for a safe voyage and for Mitch's comfort, inviting healing in whatever form God would grant. It was what the family needed. They sensed God's presence, God's peace.

The first day out was spent at sea. Mitchell spent his in bed, resting uncomfortably. Reluctantly his parents increased his medication.

Mitchell had dreamt of endless ice cream cones, winning untold prizes in the ship's arcade, playing in the ship's swimming pools, and enjoying gourmet meals—the likes of which he would prepare someday as the chef he was determined to become. Instead, he lay with subdued awareness of the stream of visitors who came calling, each whom he charged $20 to kiss his hairless head.

The second day proved much the same as passengers enjoyed Aruba, the ship's first island stop. That evening Mitch missed his third dinner. Becky sat with Mitch's grandparents and expressed the sad reality that Mitch's system appeared to be shutting down. Steve questioned if Mitch would make it home.

By Wednesday Mitchell still had consumed little nourishment, despite sumptuous meals delivered to his room, and he was showing signs of dehydration. But he seemed less agitated. As the day wore on Mitchell improved.

He had not felt good enough to visit the ship's bridge or meet the head chef and tour his kitchen. When the Captain learned why Mitch had not been able to meet him, he asked if he could come calling.

That afternoon, the classically stoic Norwegian, captain of the largest cruise ship in the world, sat with moist eyes beside the bed of the sickest but feistiest little boy he had ever met. When Steve presented him with a "T" shirt the Captain quickly understood its inscription: "It's All About Mitch."

Mitchell held his own for the next two days, sleeping by day, joining friends at dinner, and enjoying all the action on deck until late into the evening. He spent hours soaking in the hot tub cradled in the arms of his admirers. He lost money on the "slots" and enjoyed the robust sound of the poolside band. He was living his dream, for him well worth the painful price he had paid.

But, with his pain worsening, Mitchell's demeanor was changing. It became obvious by mid-day on day five that his condition was worsening again, a fact confirmed by the ship's doctor.

The doctor immediately began the paperwork necessary to secure Mitch's early departure. The captain authorized free, uninterrupted telephone use. Becky prayerfully began a long list of calls and soon the waters parted. They'd depart from St. Thomas the next day.

Mitchell ordered his only ice cream cone of the trip as paramedics arrived. Before it could be delivered, the paramedics placed him on a gurney, wheeled him to a waiting ambulance, through customs and onto a flight. One plane change later, Mitchell returned to Minneapolis, where another ambulance delivered him and Becky to awaiting care at Fairview University Medical Center on the University of Minnesota campus. Stephen's flight touched down moments later.

During the early morning hours of day seven, while Mitch's entourage slept and the ship steamed toward San Juan, Mitchell's physicians in Minneapolis confirmed the worst. Mitchell would not return to his Chanhassen home.

Chemotherapy and radiation had long been discontinued as ineffective because of Marfan Syndrome and the invasive nature of Mitchell's cancer, which was present in his body from head to toe. All that remained now for Mitch was waiting and ever-stronger medication. Friends came to comfort Mitch and his family, who were now living by his bedside........

Letting Go

I don't believe Mitchell understood the severity of his condition as he, Steve and I left our family and friends on the Island of St. Thomas, ending our cruise one day early, returning to Minneapolis and to the hospital that had become Mitchell's second home.

As Mitchell adjusted again to the hospital's daily routine, his condition worsening by the hour, my father asked, "Are you able to leave Mitchell here and go home alone?"

At the time, I couldn't accept that Mitchell would remain and I would leave without him. Throughout his numerous hospital stays, most lasting for several days as he received blood, or platelets, or Chemo, I stayed with him. Each time Steve and I brought him there. Each time Steve and I returned home with him.

Even though he had become progressively worse over time, each previous trip to the hospital had brought temporary improvement and he had been able to return home. I know he thought this time would be no different. But now it was time to accept what we feared in our hearts—this time we could return home alone.

While we had had many conversations about death, preparing Mitchell as well as ourselves, the inevitable remained a distant reality. A few days before his death, as he lay in his hospital bed, he said emphatically, "I'm not going anywhere yet!" Mitchell understood that without divine intervention he would journey to his new home with Jesus, but he was far from ready to leave his family.

On the fringe of our hope waited the miracle for which we had prayed, for which thousands of friends around the globe had prayed in faith. It simply was inconceivable that I must say good-bye...forever. But out of the depth of our love for our son and wanting only God's best for him, we knew we must let our precious son go. It broke our hearts to say, "It's okay to go."

Mitchell's Miracle Healing

Throughout Mitchell's last two weeks of life I continued to believe God could and would miraculously heal him, for such a possibility existed as long as Mitchell remained with us. Yet, such faith was in conflict with the reality I saw each passing day. Daily, I struggled with my emotions and my doubts. I feared saying good-bye. I feared the future known only to God. And I questioned, was such a healing truly God's will?

I argued within: *It seems so unfair that Mitchell must die to be healed. Why would God choose to do it that way? I'm not ready to let go of him. I don't want to give him back to God. Not yet. I don't want to say good-bye.*

I believe God performs miracles on earth as visible signs of His power and love for us. I know God desires that we know Him and His Son, Jesus. It seemed so clear to me, many would be drawn to God through a miracle, the miraculous healing of Mitch.

So I reasoned with God, "Healing Mitchell would be

an obvious sign of Your love. People would come to know Jesus and accept Him as their personal Savior. Why then would You choose to heal Mitchell in Heaven and not here? Healed here, the whole world would know."

I clung to the reality that it is within God's power to heal. So it was that, while holding onto the hope of a miracle, I continued to pray for my son. I prayed for comfort and understanding. And I asked God to help me deal with my doubt.

I also began to pray that God would prepare my heart for His perfect will. Every time I would begin to question why, I'd pray, "Dear Lord, please let my desires be Your desires; let Your desires by mine."

So it was, in the quiet of my prayers, that God's sovereign love comforted me. He reminded me that Heaven is God's best. Heaven is God's ultimate miracle, His eternal place free of pain and suffering. God wants His best for our son. While I held to the hope that God would heal Mitch on earth, I understood at last that His desire may be to heal him completely in Heaven. There it was, either place, I knew my son would be healed.

Wow! I asked God to make His desires mine, and

He did.

To accomplish His divine purpose, He will use miracles, and yes, people, too. Mitchell has a role in God's eternal purpose! Possibly, if he is healed in Heaven, many more people will be drawn to Jesus and will accept God's gift of salvation through Mitchell's story of persistent faith in the presence of discouragement. This is the ultimate miracle of Mitch!

Voyage Continues

(Excerpt from *Mitchell's Voyage Home*, by Ronald Stanchfield)

Late one evening, long after the parade of daily visitors had retired to their homes, Becky lay close to Mitch, bending from her tall, cushioned stool beside his bed. She stroked his hairless head, speckled with a fading tan from radiation to his head weeks earlier, administered to retard a tumor's incursion into his brain.

"Do you understand what's happening?" she asked.

"What do you mean?" he responded quietly.

For the moment Mitchell was feeling good. The intense pain he had been suffering was controlled by increased levels of morphine administered now from a pump under Mitch's control. Upon his return to Fairview University Medical Center, Mitchell had declared his desire to remain in the hospital rather than be cared for at home. Here was comfortable, familiar ground where doctors and nurses had become extensions of Mitchell's family.

"Your body is giving up its fight," his mother continued. "It seems God is going to heal you in Heaven, not here. This means you are going to see Jesus soon."

In the dim light they spoke quietly of his pending death. They spoke of heavenly scenes with his strength renewed, riding his bicycle on streets of gold and reuniting with great grandparents. And they wept.

"One more thing," he said after their tears subsided. "How long are they—the doctors—saying?"

"Days. Maybe a week. Maybe two," Becky answered truthfully. Then they embraced and weeping engulfed them again.

"How do you say good-bye to someone you love so very much?" Becky asked God. *"I know Heaven is a very real place and that I'll join him there in an instant of his 'forever time'. Still, I can't imagine my life without him."*

During this emotional, nocturnal conversation Mitchell expressed his growing weariness. Only the strongest medication restrained the intensifying onslaught of muscle cramps and pain (masked by the level of medication) surging deep inside his bones. He was tired of fighting.

"When you want to stop fighting, it's okay," Becky

told him. "It's okay, Mitchell. The pain you feel, all loneli-ness and sadness will disappear in Heaven. We will miss you very much. And for us it will seem a long time before we see you again. But, for you it will seem only an instant. It's okay to stop fighting, Mitchell. When you want to leave here and go to Jesus, you can go."

She knew he was fighting for her and Steve's benefit, enduring pain as much for them as for himself; they loved each other so. With God's help she could live with her pain, as difficult as that might be but, now as his mother, she needed to grant Mitch permission to let go, to not endure his pain any longer. She knew Steve felt the same.

The next day, with only Mom and grandparents in the room, Mitchell rallied again; his pain controlled by ever stronger doses of medication.

He viewed photographs that Mom and his grand-mas had brought to the hospital. They had selected several dozen to be displayed at his funeral service, preparation for which had become the pastime while Mitchell dozed.

As he returned the last photo to its pile, his mother

bent over his bed and rested her head close to his. He ran his fingers through her long, silky blond hair.

"Mom, can I go home with you?" he asked softly, obviously reflecting on the good times that had been captured by the photographs.

Becky answered as best she could—honestly. That's what he expected from her. Holding back tears, she reminded him of the previous night's conversation and of the heavenly home awaiting him.

He listened without speaking. Tears soon became visible in his eyes. But he didn't complain. She remained beside him as long as she could, until the dam holding back her tears could hold no more. Then she retreated around a corner, out of his sight, where her emotion ran its course.

Mitchell's breathing was increasingly labored due to a new tumor that had formed in Mitchell's chest cavity. As it filled with liquid, it pressed on his right lung. With each passing day he had fought for breath, while smiling at visitors and collecting a fee for each kiss planted lovingly on his shiny head. By day 12 of his hospital stay he had accumulated $800—money he intended for his mom to use to purchase jewelry, his special, final gift to her.

As evening progressed, visitation was restricted to family. Grandparents, aunts, uncles, cousins saw Mitch's occasional smile and told him they loved him—a lot. They understood the finality of their good-bye. Those who could remain did so, catching a minute of sleep on the floor in the corridor or folded into a chair in the family waiting room before resuming their vigil at Mitch's bedside where Becky, Steve, Melissa, and Mitchell's small dog, Pico, remained. Doctors removed their monitors, all indicators registering *extreme*............

Heaven's Gate

Mitchell was alert when awake during what would become his last day on earth. Doctors had increased his pain medication and his periods of sleep were longer and more frequent. Often during his sleep he would speak, responding to some scene or activity he was living in his mind.

The doctors had prepared us for this, telling us that the type and dosage of Mitch's medication could break down the barrier between conscious and unconscious thought and that talking in his sleep would be normal. Often he would awaken and say something witty. He would be very much with it and would carry on conversation and recall memories.

Shortly after midnight Mitchell began to scream. It seemed more a scream of protest than of fright. He did not want to die. He continued for several minutes. Steve and I knew Mitchell did not want to feel pain when he died. Was he in pain? We didn't understand what was happening to him. Frustrated, we could only watch as our hearts broke within us.

Eventually the doctor ordered more medication and Mitch was quiet again. I crawled onto his bed and lay beside him. With my hand upon his chest I monitored his condition. With fluid building in his lungs and a new tumor applying pressure to his right lung, breathing was difficult. But his breathing was steady. Soon I fell asleep.

While I slept, my mother came to her grandson's bedside. Responding to God's urging, she held Mitch's hand and began to pray. She thanked God for the gift of Mitchell in all of our lives. She thanked God for His grace and mercy, for His sovereign love, for the many friendships that brought great comfort, and for meeting each and every need during such a time of crisis.

"Thank you, Lord, for your ministering angels...," she prayed. Then she heard it—the melodic chorus of harps. She looked about the room for the source. The music expanded over Mitchell's bed and soon filled the room. "Do you hear the music, Mitch?"

He responded, "Uh-huh."

"I do, too," she said, and asked, "Isn't it beautiful?"

Again he said, "Uh-huh."

"Thank You that Your angels are here," she prayed. Then, as quickly as it began, the music was gone. People soon began to enter the room.

I awoke suddenly. As I lay beside Mitch an unusual sensation came over me—enveloped me. I could hear his breathing. I could feel his heart beat. But our Mitchell was no longer there. The spirit that had filled the failing body beside me was gone.

My mother asked me, excitedly, "Did you hear the music? There were harps!" I had heard nothing. Then it became clear to me that God had given my mother a most precious gift. She had heard the Gates of Heaven open for her grandson. Mitchell's spirit was in Heaven with Jesus, even while his body continued its struggle.

As morning approached, I lay beside Mitch while Steve cradled him in his arms and stroked his head. Melissa looked on. Mitch's labored breathing slowed. The rapid but strong heart beat, which I had been monitoring with my hand upon his chest, became weak. Then, in an instant, Mitchell's long, thin body, his spirit no longer in residence, shut down altogether and Mitch's pain ended at last. He was home.

Going Home

Steve, Melissa, and I drove home in silence. Leaving the hospital and going home without Mitchell was excruciatingly difficult. Waves of shock and a flood of tears left no room for words.

Arriving home, Steve and Melissa were able to enter our house. I was not—not at first, anyway. They had already processed some of the emotion they would experience this day. They had already returned home alone, knowing Mitch would never return there again. But, because I had stayed with Mitch in the hospital 24 hours a day for the last two weeks, the reality of the moment was more than I could handle.

I couldn't go in. I had considered how difficult it would be, entering our home without our Mitchie Boy, but now I had to face it. An hour later I stepped inside. As I did, memories I thought would make me happy only sickened me. Quickly, I retreated outside, not wanting to speak to anyone. Everywhere, everything reminded me of the son I wanted back.

I didn't understand what I felt emotionally. But, it was more than I could bear. I cried to God, "I have never felt this way before. It's horrible! I want it gone! Please take it away!" I felt physically sick, the pain of a broken heart.

When I finally reentered the house, my mother fixed me a cup of tea and prepared a hot bath. I climbed in and sipped at my tea, hoping it would help. The water's warmth penetrated to my inner being.   But soon, I began to feel sick again. My heart pounded. I could not escape the all-too-vivid picture of Mitch struggling to breathe as his life ended. I panicked, "I have to get out of here!"

Jumping out of the tub, I ran into our bedroom where Steve had been resting. Tears from the very core of my being broke free. I couldn't stop them. I dropped onto the bed. We cried and prayed together, and then I rolled over and began to sob.

All I could do was cry. Steve didn't know what to do. He was afraid for me; he feared that I was falling into the pit of despair, from which there would be no return.

Nonetheless, when I requested that he leave because I wanted to be alone, he left me in my misery.

Alone and in tears, I poured out my broken heart to God. I released my anger and my fears to Him. Gradually, I felt my strength return as God filled me with a new supernatural strength, empowering me to do what I could not do on my own—continue on.

Then as I thanked God for His presence, for His grace and His sovereign love, my tears began to subside. The bedroom door slowly opened. It was Melissa. Stepping inside, she looked at me and questioned, "Mom, why are you so sad?"

I moved to her. We sat on the edge of my bed and hugged. I explained how hard it was for me to come home without Mitch. She responded tenderly, "Mom, Mitch is in Heaven, and he wants you to be happy!" Her simple but wise words filled me with peace and comfort.

"You are my angel sent by God," I told her. God used my precious daughter's words to answer my prayers. Moments later, as I assured Steve that I was feeling better, I found myself distracted by a reoccurring phrase rolling through my mind like words on a marquee, "Well done my good and faithful servant!"

I marveled at how merciful God is! I realized God's Holy Spirit was speaking directly to me. God knew my troubled and broken heart, that I needed such words of encouragement. In faith I had turned to Him for strength. For this He was pleased. It was God telling me, "Well done my good and faithful servant!"

Voyage..Home At Last

(Excerpt from *Mitchell's Voyage Home*, by Ronald Stanchfield)

Three days later, Joel Johnson, pastor of Westwood Community Church, where the Chepokas family attended, addressed the crowd of 2,000, that had gathered at a church in Chanhassen to celebrate Mitchell's life.

"This is a celebration," he began. He was right. In honor of Mitch, people came dressed in festive colors. With the city's fire trucks leading the way, nearly 150 of Mitchell's classmates paraded from their school to the church on bicycles, trailing bright helium-filled balloons, which they released in unison as the service began.

Photographs and flowers were everywhere. A band played Mitchell's favorite music in the sanctuary. The atmosphere was sad but far from somber.

Finally Pastor Johnson asked, "Why did a loving God take Mitchell's young life?" "He didn't," he answered. "God made Mitchell for eternal life. His brief life was but a speck of dust in the continuum of time, his family's time on earth but the thickness of a piece of paper. For those who believe, it will be only an instant before they see him again."

Becky, Steve & Melissa agree, "It will be soon in Mitchell's *forever-time*."

Mitchell was laid to rest on Tuesday, April 15, 2003 at a small, wooded site in suburban Shorewood, Minnesota, beside his maternal great-grandparents. Helium-filled Mylar balloons were released by Mitchell's adolescent cousins at the private ceremony. The shiny balloons seemed to echo Mitch's life, as they were swept up in a gust of wind, only to be caught and entangled in nearby trees. The wind's fury at last sent them heavenward to great applause by those watching. You could sense Mitchell smiling as he looked on.

My Grief—What is it?

I awaken at night, crying. During these periods of loneliness and despair, I drown my hurt in tears. I feel numb to the world, utterly and totally lost, and frightened by my deep sense of loss. I plead with God, *What am I to do? What is grief? What is this that I am experiencing?*

To function and cope I need information. I need answers to these questions.

God answered. I was led to books that friends had given me to read for comfort. They helped me a lot. I learned I was not alone. I learned I was on a journey others had taken before me. I learned there are stages to grieving, which I, too, could expect to experience in my own way.

Sure, grieving is very personal and individualized. No two people will process their pain, their loss in the same way. But the pattern, as it unfolds in our individual lives, is similar. Like those before me, I can expect my grieving journey to last my entire lifetime. And like those before me, I will heal along the way, as I allow myself to heal.

To heal I need to be reminded of what I already know and profess—God will strengthen me for the journey. God knows and understands exactly what I am feeling each moment of each day. He knows the course before me. He knows what I need in order to continue. He will equip me for the journey. He will mold me and make me a better person.

As I read, I learned to appreciate the SHOCK, which will numb me in the beginning, shielding me as with an invisible, protective covering. I learned that TEARS will come without warning, triggered by a memory or a thought, a response to something I will hear or see. And the tears will help me to heal.

I learned that because I am uniquely made, no one else could know how I feel. There are times when I will feel very much alone, even ABANDONED. I will experience CONFUSION as I attempt to sort out in my mind the *"why"* of my loss.

I will feel GUILT and will blame myself, or my husband, for our—for my—inadequacies. I may feel guilt for the life I still have and may even refuse to feel and accept the joy which can still be mine.

But, as I accept REALITY, little by little my strength will return. Then I can, and I will, pick myself up and continue on. Through my reading, God has shown me the stages through which my grief will pass, stages with which I can measure my progress.

Daily I face many difficult emotionally-charged situations. Some I must allow to unfold and define before I can continue along a now familiar path. In other situations, I must resolve some issue before I continue.

But, none of this I do alone—for God is with me. He strengthens me daily as I allow. My grief is God's tool, and each stage is like a stepping-stone along my journey. God is molding me and making me new.

Moving Beyond Shock

As the first weeks following Mitch's death began to slowly pass, my mind, which had been numbed by disbelief during the first few horrendously difficult and busy days, began to clear. The early shock that had covered my deep emotional wounds like a bandage, had caused my old daily routine to be unimportant so that I could focus on the urgent, like arranging the funeral and attending to basic family needs. As the shock began to subside, I was gradually able to return to those *unimportant* daily responsibilities.

One chore I could no longer put off was unpacking Mitchell's suitcase from our recent cruise. I began removing new clothing he had never worn and treasures and toys he had not had the strength or time to enjoy. I was flooded with precious memories.

Suddenly, my anguish exploded. On the floor, surrounded by Mitchell's things, my heart shattered. I cried out, "I want my Mitch back! Lord, I know You are in control of my life, please guide me and give me the strength I need to endure. You created me. Only You know what I am feeling. Tell me, how do I grieve? Please help me, Lord, to understand."

After regaining my composure, I realized there was a pattern to my frequent emotional eruptions. I recognized the early stage of grieving that I had read about earlier. First was disbelief, followed by the numbing bandage of shock. But this soon ripped away exposing my emotional pain as an open sore, raw and tender.

While I wondered if God was trying to get my attention, an unexpected peace swept over me. God was answering my prayer. He had exposed my pain to grant me understanding. He was showing me, that to be healed, my pain must first be exposed. Only then can I deal with it. Then, how I grieve is my choice to make.

It was a choice He was urging me to make. If I chose to stay in a state of shock, its numbing effect would soon give way to dangerous, all-consuming self-pity and anger. I would be left emotionally crippled with a heartache I was unable to heal.

So it is, with each emotional breakdown, I must

choose to move beyond shock. To be healed, I must journey through each stage of grief. As a wound exposed to the healing qualities of the air heals more quickly, I must allow God to expose my wounded soul so that I may become whole once again.

Breakdowns will continue as sadness remains. But God will provide the strength to move beyond the numbing effect of shock.

Tears

One morning, during the first month after Mitchell's death, I longed for companionship. I had been frustrated battling my emotions. Mitch was in Heaven, healed and free of pain. I wanted to feel happy. But instead I felt heavy-hearted and empty inside. Hoping to eliminate this present pain, I sought activities that would be "normal."

I met two close friends at my neighborhood coffee shop. We sipped our favorite coffee concoctions, warmed our hands on the hot cups and began to visit, just like we had done many times in the past. But soon we sensed an invading sadness. Each of us knew this time together would not be like those happier days gone by. The topic turned to me.

As I shared with them my battle of emotions, uncontrollable tears began streaming down my cheeks. Barely able to speak, I sobbed, "I am so tired of crying. I would love to be able to get through a conversation without breaking down."

My friends thought there was nothing wrong with my crying. In fact, they were encouraged to see my tears. They expected tears, my circumstance justified tears and sorrow. There had been concern among my friends that I appeared to be too strong and together. I saw my tears as only a physical release from stress, heartache and loneliness for my son. I became frustrated when these emotions flared and tears welled up and surfaced.

As I sobbed, my friend wrapped her arms around my weary body and spoke to me through her own tears, "Becky, God gave you your emotions. He wants you to feel. You are crying because you miss Mitch and through your tears you are remembering him."

In her embrace, the fog of my heartache began to clear. God did not intend for my tears to only release my stress from jumbled emotions. There is actually a rhythm and pattern to my tears that brings me healing: Memories of Mitch make me cry. I cry because I miss Mitch. And I miss Mitch when and because I remember him. "Wow!" My tears equal remembering my son!

Instantly hope flooded my spirit. This was a "God" moment. I welcomed the filling of His love and grace. I felt overwhelmed by a new sense of release from the frustration my tears caused. He was helping me understand still another element in my grieving journey.

As each day passes without Mitch my emotional floodgate opens, releasing uncontrollable tears. But my perspective of those tears has changed. I know now my tears are another way God has given me to remember my son—now and forever.

HELP!
A Father's Plea

Coming to grips with my own loss seemed all that I could do. I was aware of Steve's pain, for certainly it was no less than my own. But I failed to understand some of his actions, for men and women grieve differently, fathers grieve differently than mothers.

I find comfort in sharing my feelings, not all the time, but much of the time. Sharing what I feel enables me to process my emotions, to get them out in the open where I can deal with them. I understand now, that is a woman's way of dealing with sorrow and grief—sharing tends to dispel or diffuse anger.

On the other hand, men tend to bury their emotions, often so deep there is no release until the pressure, the hurt, becomes too much to bear. Then the only release is explosion.

It was not long after Mitchell's death that Steve and I experienced first hand the differences in the way we

77

process our loss. Steve posted the following notable explosion on our website.

> Just when I thought I was handling things well, going about grieving the right way, it hit like a ton of bricks! Implosion! My walls came tumbling in. I raged inside! What is my purpose? Is there a purpose to anything anymore?

> It was sudden, the extreme anger I thought I had conquered. We had been out as a family, having a great time visiting friends at their home. Then, out of no-where, my torch was lit. I cried out in anger. I began yelling at the ones I loved most.

> I hated everything...everybody. My son was dead. It was no one's fault. But, he was gone. I couldn't accept that he'd be gone forever. Oh, I wanted him back. In my mind I thought he would appear. I willed him to return...the very next minute. It simply couldn't be true—he's gone forever.

> Over the course of the next hour my

grieving family ripped at each other. We tore each other apart. It was our worst night ever as a family.

Then, suddenly I realized what was happening; just how serious had become our individual struggles with Mitch's death. Grief had over-powered us. We were overwhelmed. Our grief had grown beyond our ability to cope. In our own way, each of us was trying desperately to keep control of our emotions, our hurt, and our loss, rather than leave it to God.

I am still so much a-work-in-progress Christian. It's so incredibly hard for me to give it all up, to let God take charge of my grief. I have so many unanswered questions. Like, why? Why did this have to happen to my good, fun-loving, and happy family? When will our pain become manageable?

I'm not as strong as people think I am. We're not as strong as we appear. I realize *that now. And I know Becky, Melissa and I will get through this...together! We just need a ton of prayer right now, a lot of prayer for our "Family Unit." We weren't prepared for this. It's a real struggle. We've never experienced a loss like this—it wasn't in the manual.*

That night we realized that counseling was more than a topic of speculative discussion. It was a must. It is what we need now. These times are, by far, the worst I have experienced. Our grief has taken our breath away. I cannot get Mitch off my mind. But we will see this through, together. Please help us Lord. Lead us to a professional who understands our loss. Help me.

After the anger subsided we realized God was allowing us to see our differences for what they are, perhaps unchangeable, for we are who we are, but exposed and in the open so we could deal with our loss as husband and wife, as father and mother and sibling.

My Birthday

Six weeks after Mitchell's passing I turned 39. It was a beautiful spring morning, the sun rising in the eastern sky, chasing away yesterday's clouds, drying the puddles from the previous day's cold rain.

Birds chirped their morning wake-up call as I leashed Mitchell's dog, Pico, in the front yard. I pulled a chair into the warm sun and said "good morning" to God.

Mitchell loved celebrations. He particularly loved birthdays. Birthdays were a special time to show our love and affection to each other. Each year he would help one of his grandmas bake a special cake, just for me. He'd insist upon helping open each decorated package, and then wrap himself in the paper and bows.

Today would be my first birthday in nine years without Mitch to celebrate with me. It was the beginning of a good day. I prayed, "God, grant me the strength to enjoy this special day without my son."

Later that morning, I was again alone and sought

out the warm sun shining onto our deck. I felt ready to put down on paper what I was experiencing. I prayed with pen in hand and began to journal. I continued until it was time to prepare to go out with my girlfriends, who were coming to treat me to a birthday lunch.

While I busied myself, I became aware of a change in my demeanor, a change subtle but sure. Mitchell's death had been my focus for the past six weeks. Since then I'd been looking back, counting the days as they slowly passed. But today was a milestone. Today I was looking forward, eager for a future event. It was a future without my son, but it was the future, not the past.

My special day, proved to be as special as I had hoped. It came six weeks to the day of Mitchell's death. I experienced moments of sadness and tears, but I was healing. I could feel it. Steve, Melissa and I celebrated without him. We missed Mitch very much, and each, in our own way, adjusted to his absence. We made great progress.

I crawled into bed that evening and I was strong. I'd made it through the day. I picked up my journal and began to read the portion, *Mitchell's Voyage Home*, which would become the beginning of this book. Then suddenly, I lost it, exploding in tears. I sobbed uncontrollably as raw emotion surged once again.

That empty ache, sick-to-my-stomach feeling returned. It was my birthday! I wanted my son with me. I wanted to hold him as he played with my hair and we talked about the day and dreamed about the future. I missed him so. It was more than I could bear. I cried and I prayed. Then I prayed, and prayed some more.

At last, feeling a deep urging, I picked up my journal and pen and wrote the basis of what you have just read. Then I knew, my writing would bring healing. I had taken one more step in a lifetime of steps without Mitch.

Mitchell's Stuff

Clothing, stuffed animals, blankets, toys, books, collections, drawings, stereo, video games, scooters, bike, golf clubs, movies, remote control cars, glasses ... Mitchell's 'stuff'.

I struggle with the importance of Mitch's stuff; it was all so important to him in his earthly life, but in Heaven it is worthless to him. At first the thought of getting rid of anything of his was like trying to remove Mitchell's life from my memory. I couldn't do it! I would never want him removed from my memory, but what do we do with all the stuff that made Mitchell, Mitch?

After his death we piled all his "stuff" in his bedroom and shut the door! We knew that ignoring it would not be the answer, but at the time we needed to process our loss. Steve wanted to sort through Mitchell's things a lot sooner then I was able. It was too hard for me. I would go in his room and begin crying. I would see something that would trigger a memory and the pain of missing him would become unbearable. I would leave and shut the door.

During the first month after his death the room became so full we could barely open the door. I knew the time had come to open the door to his room, and to our broken hearts. We needed to attempt to sort through the 'stuff.'

We made the first attempt with help from Mitch's grandparents. They went into his room and began re-moving the piles, little by little, bringing it down stairs where Steve & I waited to sort it into more piles. We had the 'keep' pile, the 'donation' piles, the 'give-away-to-someone-special' pile, and the 'I-don't-know-yet' pile. Finally, after a long emotional day, most of the things went back in his room, but now they were organized. We could once again walk into his room. We had begun the process. And something else happened—it became easier for me, but harder for Steve to look at all the things that Mitch enjoyed.

As days pass we attempt to remove more, a little bit at a time.   Friends and family have been able to claim something tangible from Mitchell's life, from his pile of 'stuff.' Melissa has a menagerie of treasures that remind her of her brother—Mitchell's collection of stuffed animals. Steve cherishes Mitchell's hats and Mitchell's shark tooth on a chain. I have several sweatshirts, T-shirts and hats. We've donated many items, but we've kept plenty more for ourselves.

We are each emotionally wired with the need for something tangible to hold dear as a remembrance of our precious Mitchie Boy. We have the need to cling to anything that reminds us of the life we had with him. The morning Mitchell died, minutes after his last breath, Melissa clung to several of his stuffed animals. With sadness in her eyes she asked, "Can I keep these?"

For each of us, "these" things have become our lasting treasures.

Respecting Uniqueness

Mitchell's death causes our family and friends extreme sorrow; we feel broken hearted, filled with pain. As I try to understand my own sorrow and grief I feel confused, lonely, hurt and sad...I need to be comforted. So, seeking comfort from those around me, I try to communicate my emotions. But the difficulty is that we all grieve differently, feeling and reacting to our loss in our own ways.

It is apparent that our individual, God-given uniqueness requires greater patience and respect, a respect that applies to my marriage, my family and my circle of friends.

Steve and I have moments when we express our individual grief-induced fear and anger outwardly, towards each other. Because we are uniquely made and grieve differently, these painful episodes burn with frustration as our emotions intensify and we are unable to understand the other's pain or need. A lack of respect

quickly develops, causing a great feeling of abandonment.   So, suffering, pained and lonely, we separate.

A difficult experience? Yes, extremely so! But, at
such times, I choose to retreat to God in prayer and bring
to Him my feelings of abandonment. I go to Him because
no one (including myself) knows better my exact needs.
God comforts me and repairs my broken heart, allowing a
release of my expectation that others should understand
my sorrow and grieving process. God reminds me that we
process life in unique ways and that respect for this
uniqueness is imperative to the survival of our family.

Finally, with strength renewed, in a way that only
God can do, I am ready to accept our differences. Steve
and I then apologize. Forgiving each other, we embrace
and confirm our respect for each other with the words "I
love you."

Excitedly, I can say that through this entire experience God is changing my heart. He has taught me that
when I respect each individual's uniqueness I am able to
accept them as God accepts them. I see them as God
sees them: brokenhearted and lonely—just like me.

Does Time Heal?

It seemed to take forever before time began passing once again, as though for a lifetime I'd been stuck in an emotional tide pool—waiting, waiting for an awful dream to end.

Like stagnant water heating in the sun, I was filled with unexplainable emotions, feelings boiling deep within me from which there was no escape. I could not get away.

Time stood still. An hour seemed as several days. I questioned if time was the great healer; would time heal my broken heart?

Such contrast to Mitchell's final days, when Steve, Melissa and I, along with family and friends, took turns sitting beside Mitch as he lay in his hospital bed. Then I had no concept of time. We were simply there, and I ignored the clock. I could not or would not accept how quickly each precious moment was passing. We laughed, we cried, we prayed and reminisced. Our time with Mitch was coming to an end, way too quickly.

Before I realized it, one week had passed, then two. If I ignored the passage of time, would it stop? Oh, how I wanted it to stop. I wanted enough time to absorb all that I could of my son, to take in all that he was, and to make him a part of me, forever. But, two weeks after Mitch left the cruise ship and returned to the hospital Jesus called Mitch home to Heaven to receive his miracle healing.

Suddenly he was gone.

It was then time stopped. I pleaded irrationally with God, "Time won't bring Mitch back! We won't be together again until we are all in Heaven. That will take forever. I want the pain gone and my son to be back with me, now!"

God's eternal clock kept ticking and, although I may not have been aware of time's healing quality, it was performing its work within me. Again I called out to God in prayer. Then, deep within me, my faith was assured. Just as the tide returns to fill the boiling tide pool with cool, clean water, this dreadful time, too, would pass. Now, impatiently I wait, but I rest in my faith, no longer relying on my human emotions.

Time is moving again. Weeks have given way to months. And, while my journey has only begun, I am learning to grieve and to adjust to a new life from the life I once knew. I am allowing myself to mix daily responsibilities with doses of emotional pain.

Disbelief, emotional pain, happiness, all blend into each and every day. And each day I go to God again and again. There is no way I can do this on my own. Daily, I remind myself that God is in control of my life and that He desires for me to be happy. God created me and knows me. God is the only one that can satisfy my emptiness. He is the only one that can give me strength to endure each day.

Time on earth will not remove my pain. It will only partially heal me. There will be scars that I will feel the remainder of my life. Then, as with Mitchell, will come my healing. For only God can heal me and completely remove my pain. And He will. He will heal me, too, in His perfect time, in His eternal, heavenly, forever time.

Cheese Omelet

One morning, several weeks after Mitchell had died, while pouring beaten eggs into a hot buttered pan, I listened to a surfing show playing in the background as Steve flipped through television channels. Mitchell loved to watch surfing shows on cable. I began sprinkling cheese on the egg and pictured Mitchell stretched out on the couch, watching TV as he waited for his cheese omelet. It was so real, so natural.

In that very instant my bubble burst, reality came rushing back. *Mitch isn't here! He died two months ago!* My heart tumbled into despair.

I feel silly even writing that I cried over food, but at the time the emotion associated with that smallest of memories was extremely intense and painful. Mitchell had consumed many cheese omelets in his nine-and-one-half years of life, and I had not fixed one since his death. It was a 'first' and it hurt.

We had been told that our first year without Mitch would be the hardest because of all the 'firsts.' *Of course it will be,* I thought; and I pictured big things, like birthdays, holidays, vacations, etc., *but*

God will give me the strength I need to face them.

We anticipate these big events and, as we approach them, we ease the pain by trying to have a positive outlook. I pray, "God, please help me to find happiness—without my son—in what is happening around me, so that I may enjoy what You have given me."

Oh, how I wish finding joy and happiness without pain was that easy! Truly God has given me the strength to process these 'firsts,' but I didn't realize how painful it would be, especially the 'little firsts.'

I try hard to control my thoughts associated with the big events, but the 'little firsts' come from nowhere, hitting hard and fast. These 'firsts' are what we might see, hear, smell, touch or feel which trigger memories associated with Mitch. With these memories tears flow anew as pain rips open our wounded hearts.

As our first year continues, we will experience many uncontrollable 'firsts,' big and small. I want Mitch to stay alive in my memory forever. Therefore, I must allow myself to feel each and every memory as well as the associated pain. I pray I will be filled with joy from these memories of our son. I pray, too, that throughout my life, as these 'firsts' continue, they will not hurt so deeply.

Mitchell's 10th Birthday

Steve, Melissa and I joined my extended family for a summer *Christian Family Camp* vacation during the last week of July—over the thirtieth, Mitchell's tenth birthday. Our week began with open expectations and the hope of a relaxing family time despite uncertain emotions. *Mitch was supposed to be with us celebrating his birthday— here was another 'first' without him.*

Unfortunately, when Melissa left us to stay with other campers her own age, Steve and I became frustrated and angry—our family time would be minimal. Then, as we watched the other children enjoying life, playing, laughing, crying, hugging, as they participated in various camp activities, we developed a deep loneliness for Mitch. For Steve it was a very dark loneliness, our grieving is so completely different.

My agony filled me with anxiety. It felt like a mountain, too ominous and too big to climb over. And I knew I must fight the possible crippling effects of such a flood of emotions. I knew this was part of my healing process—to be experienced in order for me to once again feel joy. So, I sought out comfort from God in many tearful sessions of prayer. I sought out companionship with family members; talking, listening, and reminiscing about Mitch.

As the week progressed, our anticipation of Mitchell's upcoming birthday grew. None of us knew how we were supposed to feel. Steve and I felt like we were on a seesaw: one side up, feeling uplifted and happy and the other side down, very low—hitting the bottom. We didn't understand our own emotions; consequently it was very difficult for anyone to help us.

The day of Mitchell's birthday had arrived. It was beyond difficult for Steve. Melissa did well, focusing on enjoying her time with her cousins. I was determined! I was determined to hit my deepest and darkest emotions head on—trusting God would strengthen me. I wanted to find joy in my memories of Mitch and I was determined to enjoy this very special day, the day that I had brought Mitch into this world.

As previously planned, our extended family met

together for lunch. Together we celebrated Mitchell's birthday. Choosing something Mitch would have liked, Steve, Melissa and I decided on pizza.

Our caravan of cars headed into the nearby town in search of the perfect pizza parlor. As we drove, we watched very dark clouds grow in the distant sky, hoping we'd arrive before the approaching rain. But, as we ran from our cars to the restaurant, the sky opened wide in a drenching downpour. We bounded through the door laughing at the sight of each other dripping with rain. Our spirits began to lift despite the frustration; *why couldn't it be sunny for our Mitchie?*

As I reflect back now, I picture Mitch up in Heaven with a gigantic squirt gun, handing one to Jesus while he laughs and says, "It's my birthday, come on, let's get'em—OK, open fire—now!" I imagine Mitch laughing, looking down from up above, as he and God soaked us completely with pouring rain.

Our restaurant of choice was small, yet quaint. Our family of 13 ordered Mitch's favorite pizza. We shared bittersweet memories of Mitch, bitter in that Mitch no longer was physically with us, but sweet because of our faith and because Mitch was with us in spirit and, because of strength from God, our family is together! To conclude our lunch Mitch's uncle Marty presented us with a framed copy of a beautiful poem which he had written about Mitch and had read at Mitchell's burial.

Throughout the day of Mitchell's birthday, Steve struggled, waging an internal battle, not allowing others to come close or enter into his pain. Melissa seemed to be receiving all the comfort she needed from her cousins and new friends. I continued my struggle to understand my process of healing, wanting it to be over and done.

Later that evening we attended Bible hour, a time set aside for bible study and for socializing with other campers. The leader, a pastor from a large, Twin City suburban church, who knew about Mitchell's death and the struggle we were experiencing adjusting, had us stand. He introduced us and invited the group to pray for our entire family. It's amazing how God always knows what we need! There is no other way to explain it than to say that, during that prayer, each of us felt the power of the Holy Spirit move through us as an unexplainable release of emotion and tears. It was God comforting us, strengthening us and healing us.

I was overcome with the realization that all the pain we were enduring was but one more step in accepting Mitchell's death. Furthermore, our willingness to allow others to join in our pain and to pray for us was God's provision for healing our broken hearts. And, because we allowed God to work through others to fill us with His healing love, those who prayed could also experience the presence of God's love.

With our hearts lightened and our emotions eased, our family concluded the day gathering at an ice cream store to indulge in another of Mitchell's favorites—ice cream. In Mitch's honor my father even had a triple scoop cone, dripping with the flavors of superman, bubble gum, and of course, cookie dough. Then, reminiscing again, we shared tears of joy as we laughed together and told goofy stories about Mitch. He will be forever in our hearts.

Wow, what a birthday—we love you Mitch!

Spiritual Peace
versus Human Emotions

PEACE. It does not mean to be in a place where there is no noise, trouble or hard work. It means to be in the midst of those things and still BE CALM IN YOUR HEART. (Author, unknown.)

These words are printed on a magnet given to me shortly after we discovered Mitch was sick. For many months it hung at eye level on our refrigerator for all to see, giving me continual inspiration, while it held in place random photos of family and friends.

Now that magnet resides in my little white, non-pill, anti-depressant that seats two and has four wheels—my convertible named, *Mitch*. On nice days I put the top down and speed away, feeling the sun warming my face and the wind flying through my hair, feeling free—enjoying what God has given me.

But there are times when this bittersweet enjoyment, this sense of freedom, is overtaken by emotion and tears trickle down my cheeks. *I miss my son and so badly want to escape the pain of my loneliness!* Trying to regain my sense of freedom I shift the gears to go faster and I speed away to escape the overwhelming agony. Then, glancing down, I see these words of peace on the magnet, and I remind myself that God is with me—He knows every ounce of my sorrow.

I cry out to God in prayer. *Why, Lord, did You have to take my son? I wanted more time with him. My faith tells me that You knew the purpose of each day Mitchell lived, and I understand that spiritually. But I hurt so much and I don't understand emotionally. Why does this have to be so hard? I cling to Your promise of love and the peace You give my spirit. But please, Lord, help me to balance what I know spiritually with what I feel emotionally! I pray that You will meet my needs and give me the strength I need to get through each day without Mitch.*

I contrast the peace God gives me with the human emotions I battle daily and to the freedom I feel in my little car and to the pain I try to escape by speeding away. It is so very frustrating to have a spiritual under-standing of God's purpose for taking Mitch, and still be consumed by such crippling emotion.

At times it seems my sorrow creates within me conflicting emotions, a tug-of-war cycle pulling me back and forth between spiritual happiness and human loneliness. This emotional tug-of-war could wound my inner self so deeply that it would destroy who God wants me to be.

To balance my grief and escape this emotional cycle, I focus on what I know to be spiritually true. I go back to God in prayer. There, God reminds me that He gave my feelings to me, but He does not expect me to function on emotions alone. God wants me to invite Him along on my journey. God wants me to feel what I feel, but in His presence and then, with an open heart, accept all that He desires for me.

I believe the Lord hears my prayers, even though He does not remove my pain. He comforts me with a peace and understanding that His plan is better then what I might imagine. I am assured that Mitch was created for a purpose, a purpose that was fulfilled here on earth and continues to be forever in Heaven.

I pray, *Thank you, Lord, that in the quiet of prayer I can come to You with the pain of my human emotions.*

Thank You for showing me how to balance these emotions with Your spiritual peace.

I reflect back to when Mitch was a baby, the nights I rocked him to sleep. He was warm and content in my loving arms, and I would sing quietly to him, "Jesus loves me this I know, for the Bible tells me so. Little ones to Him belong, we are weak, but He is strong. Yes, Jesus loves me..." Jesus loves me!

I am weak and struggle with my human emotions. But, I can experience strong spiritual peace because...Jesus loves me.

Friends

I once read in a book that a jetty is a barrier built at the mouth of a harbor to protect it from the destructive force of the ocean's crashing waves. As I look back upon my journey of life, I see how God has protected me with many jetties, one of which is friends.

Mitchell's terminal illness, death and my grieving have all brought enormous, powerfully destructive waves into my life. One of these waves is loneliness. There are times when the pain of Mitchell's death has made me very lonely. I know my friends feel the loss of Mitch. They're grieving, too. *But their loss isn't the same as what I feel*, I tell myself, as I begin to isolate myself from them. *My friends can't truly understand.*

My spiritual enemy loves this destructive emotional pattern, which I can so easily fall into. He loves to jump into this crashing wave and fill me with negativity, anger and doubt, even depression. This enemy loves it when my loneliness becomes very intense. He delights when I withdraw from my friends.

Separate and conquer. This enemy incites me to feel it's unfair that my friends can move on with life without me, that they can never understand my pain and experience that which is uniquely mine. So I withdraw and become angry. Angrier still that my friends don't even know how badly I need them.

But thank God for His sovereign, never-failing love. For it's in these angry, lonely times when God steps in, and His Holy Spirit quietly reminds me that He is always there for me. He has never left me. Even though I had pushed Him aside, too, with my own self-indulgent pity party, He lovingly reminds me that, while I don't understand how even He can help me, He is there for me. It is up to me to call out to Him, my Savior.

It's only then, when, out of my pain, I get on my knees and pray, when I humbly cry out to God, that these destructive waves crashing into my life are suddenly calmed. God does not want me to be lonely. So He humbles me and gives me the strength to call out to my friends whom He has provided. Or, He will work in them to call out to me. These friends are God's provision.

Surely, they cannot know my pain, ever, unless I share it with them. They cannot comfort my hurt unless they know it exists. God has built for me a jetty...my friends.

I am so very fortunate to have the friends I have, God given gifts. I want to appreciate my friends to the fullest. I love all the fun times we enjoy. I love their sincerity and honesty. I love their support and encouragement. I love the spiritual and emotional journey that we are on, together. I love that God has brought me friends to help me in my pain.

Thank you, Jesus, for my friends!

A Sibling's Sorrow

"How is Melissa?" well-meaning people often ask. I answer, "Considering all she is dealing with, pretty good."

We woke Melissa abruptly from a deep sleep as she lay on a roll-a-way bed beside Mitchell, just as Mitchell took his last breath. She stood in shock as we embraced and prayed our final prayer over her brother's still body and when, minutes later, the look in the doctor's eye clearly declared Mitchell was gone.

Clinging tightly to one of Mitch's stuffed animals still warm from contact with Mitch's body, Melissa returned to her bed. Her body went limp. I wrapped my arms around her and held her tight. Quietly, she anguished, "Why didn't Jesus take me instead? Is he really healed now, in Heaven? Is this how Jesus decided to give Mitch his miracle? Do you think Pico (Mitchell's dog) knows he's gone?" I don't recall my answer, but I clearly remember thinking, "Thank you Lord, she's asking questions!"

Does anyone truly know what to expect from a

very social, charismatic and emotional 13-year-old girl whose world has been tragically disrupted by the death of her little brother, one of her best friends?

Melissa misses her brother dearly. To compensate, she keeps busy with friends, movies, more friends, shopping, and more friends. At the same time she displays a growing, *seeking-independence* attitude, so normal for a girl her age. It's under great emotional pressures that she must adjust to becoming a single sibling. How does she do that? What are we to expect of her?

It is often difficult for her to talk openly about the death of her brother. So we try to tune into her actions, good or bad, as daily we try to understand just how our precious daughter is doing. We work at reading her verbal and non-verbal expressions. Actions can speak louder then words!

We've learned that her normal, w*hatever,* attitude means she is avoiding her emotions because they hurt and she doesn't know how to deal with them. Then we ask questions, lots of them, and we carefully and patiently listen. As Steve says, we reel her back in. Then our family time becomes more focused.

Together we discuss how to work through the bad and encourage the good that we see in her behavior. Most important, we love her and accept her with wide-open arms. It's with all our imperfections that we grieve together, and together we will become a stronger family.

With anguish I watch the pain and sorrow our daughter must endure as she adjusts to a life without Mitch. The mother in me would love to make it all better. Then I remember that she is God's child, too, and God has a plan for her, as well as for me. Sorrow is also a part of Melissa's journey.

I am grateful for the questions Melissa asked when Mitchell died and for the questions she continues to ask. I pray for guidance and patience and ask God to make Steve and me aware of Melissa's needs and to know how to meet them.

Excitedly we watch as our wonderful daughter grows into the women that God intends her to be.

Christmas

Our family loves all the excitement and pleasures of Christmas and the joy the season brings. I remember past Christmases, beautifully decorated trees glistening with ornaments and twinkling lights, and carefully wrapped presents tucked underneath. I remember the aroma of fresh-baked cookies filling the house, and festive gatherings with family and friends... *Now,* I asked myself, *will we be able to enjoy these wonderful Christmas experiences again, without Mitch?*

As we considered the approach of this first Christmas without our Christmas-loving boy, uncertainty stirred our emotions. We even talked about traveling. Perhaps our holiday would be more enjoyable if we removed ourselves from the familiarity of home. Removing ourselves from the source of memories, possibly our pain would be removed too.

Quickly, I realized how irrational this thinking was. We could not remove ourselves from our pain by leaving.

Actually, if we left, we would seperate ourselves from those that could comfort us. And we hadn't even considered other family members who would be grieving, too. What would it do to them if we were gone?

We decided for the sake of comforting each other, it would be best to stay close to home. I also felt there was another reason to stay home, a reason not really clear at the time. It was important that we stay close to our traditions and go through this Christmas holiday in the same way we had in the past.

Melissa looked forward to our family's traditions, while Steve wanted the holidays to pass quickly, so as not to experience the pain of past memories. I stayed very busy doing all the normal activities, not realizing at the time that I was hoping I would be too busy to acknowl- edge my deep sadness.

With three weeks remaining till Christmas, I woke early one morning, prompted by a mental list of all I needed to accomplish. While still in my pajamas, I found the containers labeled "Christmas Stuff" and began sifting through 16 years of family holiday memories, amazed at all we had accumulated. Then turning on some quiet seasonal music, I began to decorate.

Looking for a specific decoration, I opened a different container. Its contents sent a wave of shock through my entire body. It was Mitchell's Christmas stocking, new last year. Wrapped inside was a snow-globe, one of his favorite decorations.

I sat on the floor, frozen with sadness and barely able to breathe. My emotions exploded and tears streamed down my cheeks. I clutched his stocking with its contents, holding it close, remembering Mitch and the joy he had felt when he saw the globe for the first time. I remembered the twinkle in his eye at the sight of the snow falling inside the magical sphere, remembering... There I sat, on the floor, my son's Christmas treasures lying on my lap, and I trembled.

Later that morning, Melissa joined me at decorating. As she took out the Christmas stockings she asked, "Mom, would it be okay if I used Mitchell's stocking this year?" Delighted at the thought of Melissa also wanting to hold close her brother's memory, I agreed.

A short while later Steve joined us and together we drove to the tree lot in search of a tree that would have met Mitch's approval. Returning home, we strung the outside lights and began decorating the tree. Our time together was charged with emotion. Whether sad, happy, angry or joyful, we allowed it all. It needed to be felt— as difficult as it was. It needed to be.

A few days later I declared the decorating done. This year, decorating would be simpler, emotionally easier and just as pretty. Now it was time to bake.

I love to bake and, the kids—most certainly Mitch—had always joined me in this holiday tradition. We would spend many hours creating treats as edible gifts to give to family and friends on Christmas Eve. This year I tried and tried and tried to enjoy my time in the kitchen. But, with each attempt to bake something my joy was disrupted by tears from one reoccurring, haunting and agonizing memory.

I could see in my mind Mitch baking cookies last year. He was so very happy. He was alone and, as he worked in the kitchen, I had approached Melissa and asked her why she wasn't helping him. I thought she should be in there too, creating memories with her brother. She answered quietly and very matter-of-factly, "Mom,

Mitch loves to bake and this will probably be his last Christmas, so I am letting him do it."

"His last Christmas." Those words kept repeating in my head, "His last Christmas." They wouldn't stop. Anxious and robbed of joy, I sobbed. Then, completely frustrated by my recurring memory and the pain it brought, I cried out, "What is happening? Why? God, please help me understand!"

When calm returned, I understood. Last Christmas, even though I knew it might be Mitch's last, I had not lived in sorrow. Then, I had wanted to enjoy every bit of it. Mitch, with his entire family, had needed to experience Christmas—his last if that was what it must be—to its fullest.

Therefore, this Christmas I must fully acknowledge that last year was Mitchell's last Christmas with us. In so doing, I must first feel the pain of my memories. Then the void caused by Mitch's absence can be filled. Only then can I embrace the past and enjoy the present.

Realizing this, I sensed healing taking place within me. I had developed a new acceptance of Mitchell's death. I was able to acknowledge that Mitch is in Heaven, where he is celebrating Christmas with Jesus each and every day, not just once a year. It also became clear to me that I could not base any happiness experienced during the holiday season on my ability to overcome sadness and pain. Rather, it should be based on the reason for the season, Jesus' birthday.

Furthermore, I began to recognize that Jesus wants me to rely on Him continually for my strength and peace. He wants me to live calmly, even with my pain and all the busyness of the holiday season. And, above all, He wants me to be happy with the present.

This Christmas was a very large FIRST. I am extremely grateful that we did not run away to escape its associated emotional pain. As Christmas day came and went, our entire family was able to comfort each other and experience healing. I believe we needed to experience this holiday, living as close to past tradition as possible, so that the emotional hole in our hearts would be filled with new joy and strength, the kind only God can give. Then, we can enjoy all our Christmases to come.

Now, that's a gift!

Competent Counseling

Even healthy, well-functioning families prove that it is our very human nature that is often the cause of tension or difficulty. As our family advanced through life, I thought we were dealing fairly well with our imperfections, managing our differences and blending our lives together. We were a diverse but happy family. That is, until the death of Mitch!

Mitchell's death made us aware of our uniqueness in ways we had not previously imagined, to the extent that our grieving has exaggerated, even aggravated our flaws. Our grieving has exposed unacceptable behavior in ways that could divide our family, creating dysfunction. Steve and I have acknowledged that we do not have the education or background to resolve our growing issues ourselves. Mutually committed to our marriage and believing it is secure in God, we sought and found a professional grief counselor. His divine guidance has led us to a counselor who, we believe, is supportive of our family and who has become an instrument for our healing.

Our goal, as husband and wife, is to grieve together

so we can be a safe and strong family, not separated and alone. As simple as it sounds, it is really difficult. It's difficult to cry together. It's difficult to quietly listen to the other's feelings without trying to fix them. As we expose our pain to each other, we become and feel very vulnerable.

We are encouraged, knowing experientially that God is very real and present in our lives, strengthening us along life's way.   We struggle as we learn why we respond the way we do, but together we are learning how to blend our contrasting emotions for our family's good.

Similarly, Steve and I are doing our best to help Melissa. We are vigilantly praying for her, watching and listening to her needs. She grieves differently then we do and we may not be able to give her the counsel she needs. So, along the way, she, too, will meet with a professional. Thankfully, God knows exactly what her needs are and who will come alongside her to help. We believe with all our heart that God will provide us with what we need to help and guide her.

While, no doubt our grieving will continue the remainder of our earthly lives, I believe God will use all of our struggles, and the helpers who come alongside, for His greatest good.

Wonderment

Our enormously difficult first year without our Mitchie boy is coming to an end with only seven weeks remaining until the one-year anniversary of his death. I don't understand why, but my emotions are strangely stable and strong. Yet, while this is true, I continue to cry, but I have noticed a new pattern to my sessions of tears.

...I glance out my window to see beautifully large and fluffy sparkling snow falling outside as children play. There are Mitchell's friends and they laugh and toss snowballs as they build a snow fort. I picture Mitch loving the freshly-fallen snow, digging and laughing with his friends. I feel that knot tighten in my stomach and tears well up in my eyes. I miss him so much. My thought wanders to where Mitch is now, in Heaven, and I wonder, *does Heaven have snow? What does Mitch love to do there?*

...Driving up the street from our home, I follow the curve of the road to see the school Mitchell attended. It's morning and children are arriving for a new day. Approaching an intersection, I see the young crossing guard all bundled in his warm winter jacket with his hat pulled down tight. It's Mitchell's buddy. Giving him a quick wave I think, *Wow, he is growing up!* Again, I feel that knot return to my stomach and tears cascade down my cheek (as they are this very moment). I wonder, *what would Mitchell look like if he were still here, changing and growing-up? Would he be a crossing guard, too?*

...My anticipation builds for our upcoming spring break vacation, sunny and warm. We will embark on a cruise ship with a family who had accompanied us one year ago, on Mitchell's last cruise, and with others who loved our son. The thought of adults and children planning their adventures brings me sadness as I wonder *what adventure Mitch would be planning for this trip. Would he be excited about where we are going?*

...I wonder so many things. I wonder about Mitch's unmet earthly expectations and those he has now in Heaven. These are my sessions of wonderment! This is my time to reflect on the life Mitch had here with us, and allow myself to feel the pain of missing my son's loving companionship.

My tears flow with each memory of Mitchell's hugs and of him playing with my hair. Knowing that Mitch is in Heaven where Jesus is, I pray, "*Hey Jesus, will you do me a favor? Will you please find Mitch for me and give him a huge hug. Tell him it's from his mom and that I love him. Please, Lord, let my precious Mitchie boy know that I miss him so much. Tell him I can't wait to be with him again, forever in Heaven! Thank you, Jesus. Love, Mitchell's mom, Becky*"

Emotions of Uncertainty

Now, nearly one-year after Mitchell's death, I find myself reliving in my mind that dreadful time that became the final two weeks of his earthly life. The difference is, I know all the answers to the once very frightful questions associated with each flaunting memory now making its way through my mind.

In spite of the benefits of hindsight, each memory brings new anxiety, stirring and agitating my inner self, tying a knot in my stomach. I ache inside and my chest pounds while this anxious knot moves up through my throat only to emerge in an uncontrollable flow of tears. I want to scream, *why? What am I feeling? Why do I feel this way now after so much time has passed? I want to understand.*

Finally, it has become clear that these current emotions are actually the explosive feelings associated with the uncertainty triggered by each memory of last year and the unfathomable questions that crashed down upon me in powerful waves during that time of desperation. *Is Mitch dying now, here on our vacation and while on his cruise? How do we get him home to the hospital, off a cruise ship in the middle of the South Caribbean? Will his weakened body survive the two airline flights home? How long will he be in the hospital? Will he come home with us? How much time do we have left with our son? Will God heal him here or in Heaven?*

With each question I had prayed, *Lord, You know what Mitch needs and what will happen. You are the only one that knows all the answers to these questions that fill my mind. I know that in You I will have the strength to get through this. Please open my mind to know what it is that You want me to do.* God answered that prayer. He filled me with a supernatural power, a kind of superhuman emotional strength that enabled me to cope. It was as if God pushed the "pause button" to my fearful emotions, putting them aside until a day when it would be safe for me to feel them in full, a day that, one year later, has come.

But at the time, that emotional block was exactly what I needed. If I had been allowed to feel all the fear and pain associated with each new circumstance, each unknown and unseen event unfolding before me, I would not have been able to function or accomplish all that needed to be done.

God gave me the ability to pass through each situation as it opened before me with a supernatural peace, quickly filling my mind with positive thoughts of assurance and action: *I don't know the answers, only God does. I can't get emotional, so I won't go there... yet! I know the time will come, when I will have to deal with this reality. But right now, I need to "do" not "feel"!*

So, whether I like it or not, I must once again accept the undeniable fact that God has made His plan certain. Mitchell's earthly life was completed with a miraculous but heavenly healing. God has now released the "pause button" on my emotions. The time has come for me to feel those suppressed emotions, and feel them all!

So it is, one year later, my dreams come as restless sessions in the night. I sense I'm trying to resolve my grieving, trying to feel better. I only wish my dreams would give me a glimpse of Mitch! Just a glimpse! I am tired, and feel I am growing more tired each day. I feel a temporary,

129

mild depression setting in.

A severe and deep aching loneliness (a very real pain) is crippling me more each day. It is as though I have ever-new feelings of fear, fear of losing my son. I loath such fear, I loath living with such fear. My memories are filling me with anxiety, frustration and tears.

Still I believe how I feel is part of the healing cycle. Therefore, I will use this time to call upon Jesus for the strength I need. I once wrote in my journal, *my weakest human trait—depression—is a time of my greatest spiritual strength.* God seems to know I will use this time to call upon Him for comfort, peace and understanding. And this will follow as renewed strength from Him, the strength I need to be healthy.

In order to be emotionally whole, I must feel "all" of the emotions, even the year-old ones. I recognize the stages of grief with which I must engage as our first year without Mitch nears completion. And, in spite of my present reenact-ment of past events, I know I will heal fully with the ability to hold and cherish all my wonderful memories, memories of our precious time together.

Lord, I thank You for Your strength to heal. My hope rests in Thee!

One Year Later

"Good-bye!" Although we say these words daily as we conclude our time with others, they now echo with great finality because my son has died. But is the "good-bye" I said to Mitch one year ago really final? Not really. Not for me, because God promises eternal life. Still, even though one year has passed, I must make a conscious decision each day to remind myself of this truth. I try to think of it as Mitch being away on a very long vacation and that some future day will bring us together again. Forever! Then my good-bye becomes temporary.

While we are apart, I will hold close memories that will keep Mitch alive in my heart; his goofy jokes and the twinkle in his eyes, his sensitive spirit and countless other qualities. I will look forward to that day when we gather in Heaven, when I will see at last every bit of who God created Mitch to be.

I am reminded of a story a friend told me the week after Mitchell's death. He had asked a family member, whose thirteen-year-old daughter had died, what she wished others would have done differently to help her. She explained how she wished those around her would stop being afraid to talk about her loved one, because she needed to talk about her and remember her. So, his advice to me was: "Tell everyone to talk about Mitch!"

Well, Steve and I have done just that. We encourage those around us to tell us their memories and stories of Mitch. We need these memories of Mitch; they remind us of him and help us feel closer to him. Even though at times these memories can be very painful, because they remind us of his absence, it would be more harmful to our healing process if we would not allow ourselves to remember.

As this first year comes to a close, I'm aware that my journey has taught me many lessons. Some fairly easy, like reminding others to talk about Mitch, but most have been extremely difficult, like learning how I must live with the emotions of missing my son, that sense of loss that comes with all the memories.

I have learned a major lesson in the fact that I

don't go through each stage of grief in order, completing one before moving on to the next. Rather each new situation, each flash of memory or each pained emotion, may trigger one or several stages of grief. The sense of shock, tears of sadness, feelings of abandonment, confusion or guilt may reoccur over and over again. The time it takes to understand what's happening, and to accept it, may be anywhere from several seconds, to minutes, to hours, days or even weeks.

I have learned to recognize that each emotional experience may actually be my response to continuing grief. I must remain aware of that. And I must acknowledge and identify the emotion and its cause for what it is: anger, frustration, loneliness, sadness. I must be watchful of how I am relating to those around me and not blame others for how I am feeling.

I believe that for me part of God's healing is my being able to admit my feelings. Then to resolve my feelings I might talk to someone, cry, go out, rest, or get busy with something. But always I go to God in prayer for the strength only He can give. Then, and only then, can I be emotionally healthy, aware of what I need to function in life and become a stronger person. Only then will I be able to accept Mitchell's death and, with joy, move on to experience the peace and hope God desires for me.

Time may ease the severity of the pain caused by lessons I still must learn. But time will not lessen the ache in my heart or erase that grotesque scar that marks the void in my life once filled by Mitch. As difficult as it is to understand, I believe my living with this continual ache is part of God's plan for me. For living with the loss on my own is beyond my human capability. God knows that, through my sense of loss, I will continue to come to Him for companionship. This adds depth to our relationship.

This very painful experience has expanded my faith. God has granted me new abilities. He is teaching me to persevere in my faith even through the deepest, heartbreaking emotional pain. He is teaching me to cling to my memories of Mitch and that, throughout the days and years to come, I can rely on God to strengthen me and guide me along life's path.

As the end of this first year without Mitch approached, this heart-wrenching one-year anniversary of Mitchell's death, Steve, Melissa and I determined not to focus on our misery. We wanted to remember this day as positively as possible, to picture Mitch in Heaven, completely healed and enveloped in Jesus' embrace. That took no end of relying upon God.

We chose to refer to the day of Mitchell's death as his 'heavenly birthday!' We encouraged family and friends to do the same. This year we were surprised when that day fell on Easter Sunday. Wow, what a memorable coincidence, the day we gathered to remember Mitchell became the same day we celebrated the resurrection of Jesus Christ into Heaven.

We spent the day with our immediate family, enjoying a wonderful meal. We visited Mitch's grave and watched Mitchell's sister, Melissa, and Mitchell's cousins hunt for candy Easter eggs. I found the day both enjoyable and sad, although the tears I shed were not for Mitch. My tears were for everyone Mitch had to leave behind, including me. Because, we are the ones living with the sorrow that darkens our daily activities and robs us of the joy God intends, like a spring storm shadows the earth and sends a chill into the air.

Thankfully, throughout that day, my grief was

balanced by the message of Easter—the Son has risen! It was as if the sun's rays parted the ominous clouds of my sorrow, warming me within, allowing me to remember and to be thankful that my son is in Heaven. My son, too, has risen! He is celebrating eternity with Jesus.

For this reason alone, one year after my son's death, I am able to say, *Good-bye Mitch! Until the day when we are joined once again, together in heavenly forever time, we love you! All the way to Jesus and back.*

Editor's note: The phrase, "All the way to Jesus and Back," are words Mitchell spoke to his mother to express his great love for her. He was three years old.

Preparation

I often consider the length of time Mitchell lingered. It was as though God gave us extra time to ask our hard questions; time to discover some of the answers, time to prepare ourselves for the inevitable loss and sorrow. We had time to prepare Mitchell for the mystery we call death.

We feel sadness for those who have no time for such preparation. Our timeless God allots to each of us a portion of time. It is during this time, while we are alive, before death strikes, when we are to consider our ways and to prepare for our eternal life. The time of our living is the time of our eternal preparation.

I am grateful for the gift of godly parents who, despite life's challenges, worked out their faith in full view of their children. Through the trials they faced and their faith, which sustained them, I learned of a loving God who provides for His children. As I look back, I see God was preparing me for today.

God has also granted me a loving husband, a

caring daughter, supportive extended family, compassion-
ate friends and many praying strangers. These have sustained me. They, too, have helped prepare me. "Thank
You, Lord, for giving me the capacity to appreciate all that
You have given me!"

You see, I am the fortunate beneficiary of God's
preparing His own. But this is not only my good fortune. It
is yours as well. If I seem more fortunate than others or to
have greater faith with which to prevail against our sorrow, it
is because God granted me preparation time. This is God's
gift for all His human creation. He prepared me through
circumstance, upon which I can look back and see His divine
guidance. He is doing the same for you.

Steve's and my distress is not in the lack of time
allotted to prepare our family, to prepare Mitchell for his
death, but in second-guessing that we might have used the
time we had more wisely. But we cannot change the past.
We cannot undo our failures. Therefore, we find joy is in
knowing—in believing—we did the best we could. And we
move ahead in gratitude for each moment in time God may
grant us. And we seek God's guidance to use each moment
wisely, for today prepare us for our tomorrow.

Life After Death?

Perhaps life's most difficult and emotionally painful experience is the loss of a loved one. Whatever the relationship, when love is present, the pain of loss is undeniably intense and severe.

Still physical death is one of life's certainties. The Bible says it this way: "It is appointed to man once to die, then comes the judgment." Millions of people die every day. Most will leave behind someone who loves them, someone who will grieve their loss.

Mitchell died leaving many behind who grieve his loss. What makes the loss of Mitchell bearable for us, the family he left behind, is the confidence that he is in a better place, free from suffering and pain. As Heaven's gates opened to him, he was instantly healed. Furthermore, we know that we will again enjoy his company, see again his smile and hear his laughter. This will come to pass for each of his family, all in God's perfect time.

We find comfort in believing that Mitchell is experiencing a wonderful life after death, a life that cannot be compared to the life he knew here on earth, for it is far better than we could ever imagine.

We are comforted in knowing that we must endure separation for only a short period of time. Considered against the backdrop of eternity, it will be but a moment before we reunite with him in God's forever time.

Because we are comforted in this way, we are able to continue our earthly life without our beloved Mitchell. Because we have this hope, we can enjoy a life—our life—after Mitchell's death.

My greatest joy and comfort is in knowing Jesus Christ paid the price of Mitchell's admission into Heaven. When the gates of Heaven opened and we said good-bye to Mitch, he heard God say, "Welcome home!"

One Small Life

"Ready?" asked Steve. Becky looked his way, smiled warily, tugged on the door latch and stepped onto the parking lot. At the front of the car she waited for Steve. Together they walked toward the restaurant for a meeting with two of Mitchell's doctors to learn answers to the questions which had taunted them for the five months since Mitchell's death.

Steve had asked for the meeting, Doctors Wiegel and Chloisy suggested the setting, Maynard's Restaurant on the shores of Lake Minnetonka, a favorite of Mitchell's for Sunday brunch. Steve and Becky had not been to there since Mitchell's death.

They loved Mitchell's doctors, a deep emotion they felt for each staff member who had become so important to their lives during Mitchell's tornadic illness. Doctors Brenda Wiegel and Denis Chloisy had been Mitchell's primary physicians. Both were leading University of Minnesota researchers at Fairview University Medical Center, as well as practicing physicians. Both had a heart for children.

Steve and Becky were happy to see the Docs. They'd been through a lot together and had developed a strong mutual respect for one another. From the beginning their relationship had been frank, honest and to the point. That's what Steve and Becky had asked for and the Docs came through for them. (Mitchell's doctors had always told it like it was, the good and the bad while leaving room for hope—miracles do happen.)

Words cannot describe the devastating heartbreak experienced in Mitchell's room that morning of April 11, 2003. His lifeless body lay still upon his bed, his dog Pico laying at his feet. Mitchell was suddenly present with his Lord.

Mitchell had escaped the bonds of time and had stepped into God's *forever time*. But time nagged its importance and demanded delicate procedures be implemented quickly to confirm viability of specimens which Steve and Becky had agreed to make available for research. His family was asked to step out of the room. The necessary surgery would occur later and the results would remain a mystery.

Mitchell's funeral was the last time Steve or Becky had seen Mitchell's doctors. They hoped at last to learn the results of the research and whether or not Mitchell's one small life was making a difference.

Dr. Chloisy was waiting for them inside at a table. Steve and Becky pulled out chairs and seated themselves. Minutes later, Dr. Wiegel arrived.

Both Docs were delighted to meet with Steve and Becky. "You have given a most precious gift," confessed Denis. "In fact, what you have done is extraordinary. Seldom do we have a continuing dialogue with the families of deceased patients." Most families want to forget and get on with their lives as best they can, retaining only good memories. But then, most deceased children are not the subject of ongoing research.

"Mitchell's life was a gift," agreed Steve. "We miss him. It's been five months." He looked at Becky. "We need to know, what has become of this precious gift?" His tone reflected the anxiety waging war in his mind. Recently, grief-driven, he had contacted the director of the funeral home—a personal friend—to confirm that it was Mitchell's entire body that had been prepared for burial. And, of course, it had been.

"We know. And we understand," responded Dr. Wiegel, sympathetically.

"We're very sorry for the lack of communication," apologized, Dr. Chloisy. "This is new to us. As I said, what you did was extraordinary. No one has ever done this before."

Within a few minutes the doctor's demeanor was boiling excitedly. "Would you like to see what we've learned so far?" he asked.

"Of course," responded Becky, seeking closure. Mitchell had been a gift to the world. She knew that with all her heart. She looked at Steve. "Please, continue."

"The wheels of research and progress turn slowly...very slowly." He produced a tablet and started to sketch, speaking as he did. The form of Mitchell's Osteosarcoma had been different from any other their team had previously witnessed, appearing first as a single bone lesion and then spreading voraciously to permeate his entire body.

The tablet filled with diagrams of genes and

chromosomes, muscles, bones, neurons and nerve pathways as Dr. Chloisy described the miraculous nature of the research that would result from the cherished samples of bone and tissue they had removed. Because Mitchell had not had surgery to remove diseased portions of bone, his nervous system was intact, unaffected by the body's response to the trauma of surgery. This fact alone could lead to medical discoveries they had not dreamed possible.

Much of the previous research had been limited to laboratory animals and small microscopic samples. New instruments were now being tooled to process their new samples, pure and unviolated. Miraculously, the wheels of progress will run faster, remedies and cures will be discovered. Yes, it was all very miraculous, because of Mitchell's one small life and his parents' large faith.

All life has purpose. The God of the universe created life. When we look about the universe, we become aware of its organization and its enormous complexity. It's natural to wonder what role we may have in such a plan. We seem so small and insignificant.

But are we insignificant? The Bible tells us that we

are created in the very image of the God of the universe. That being the case, we should not feel insignificant. Why then, if we are significant to God, does He allow pain and suffering? Does He care about that which He created?

The life of Mitchell Chepokas is proof that God cares. God's love is manifest in the way in which God can and does create good out of bad. Mitchell's insidious cancer will ultimately produce good, as research of his disease and its cure becomes known.

Mitchell has been granted new life, a new life in God's *forever time*. A true life free of suffering and pain, forever! Now we see the one small life Mitchell endured, he unknowingly lived for others, so that God's creation on earth might someday live a better life.

So it is that those whose lives Mitchell touched so deeply can say, "Good-bye, Mitch. We'll see you soon. Thank you for your gift of life, your whimsical smile, your silly humor, your faith. In an instant of your *forever time*, we'll be with you again."

Birth of a Miracle

Beyond the doors of Fairview University Medical Center, people huddled against winter's wind, their spoken words visible as ghostly puffs of vapor. Patients, staff, visitors streamed in and out, some working, some attending some class, and others visiting patients on the floors above. Some of those being visited would not see Christmas, now just weeks away.

Mitchell would see this Christmas. Of that he was certain. His family and friends had scheduled a Caribbean cruise for March and death would not steal it away. Doctors agreed.

In Mitchell's room on 5B, Steve sat beside Mitchell's window, his fingers entering an update of Mitchell's condition into his laptop to be read by the thousands of supporters who daily logged onto Mitchell's website. It was Steve's turn to live-in with Mitch so that Becky could prepare for the holiday season. This was yet another of Mitch's five-day treatments, which doctors hoped would impede the destructive growth of his cancer.

Mitchell lay on his bed as the muted television

played Animal Planet, its sound streaming from the hand control resting on Mitchell's pillow near his ear. He watched and smiled as a nurse entered his room with a brightly decorated package. The attached card said it was from a friend.

Mitchell loved receiving gifts from his friends. He had no shortage of either. He eyed the package pensively for several minutes. Finally he asked, "Dad, why do I have so much and so many other kids here have so little?"

"You have lots of friends, Mitch, people who love you," answered Steve as he looked up from his keyboard. He wondered if he saw tears in his son's eyes.

"People love them, too," Mitchell corrected, somewhat defensively. Then, thinking for a moment he added, "No one brings the other kids gifts like this, not like I get."

"Mitchell, God has blessed you. Our family is blessed. What can I say? How can I say it? You have many friends. These friends want to show you their love. And they can do that by giving you something that will make you feel good. We live close by, and so do our friends. Some of the families, whose kids are here, come a long way and can't come as often. They have too far to travel. And many can't afford gifts."

That wasn't entirely what was bothering Mitch. "Dad, it's Christmas. These families need help."

"You're right, Mitch. They do," agreed Steve.

Over the course of Mitchell's treatment Steve had come to know many families at the hospital who had paid beyond their resources in their medical crisis. Some were unable to make house and car payments. At the risk of losing everything back home, some traveled great distances and at considerable expense to obtain the treatment they hoped and prayed would heal their child, or keep alive a little while longer. For the kids in these families, their only gift is their parents' love.

"So what do you want to do, Mitch?" Steve asked.

Mitchell didn't answer immediately, but finally asked, "How much money do I have, Dad?"

"Well, Mitch," Steve began thoughtfully, "Our last fund raiser raised $25,000." This money would help considerably to pay medical costs that went beyond the scope of their very good medical coverage. For Steve, this was one way in which God had blessed.

"I don't mean that money. How much do I have?"

Steve thought of their growing list of friends and

contributors. Blessed indeed. These were people, following Mitchell's story through the website, whose hearts God touched with an urgency and an eagerness to give. Most gave money, and most was designated for "non-insured" expenses. But some sent money with instructions, "For Mitch to use any way he wants." Some specifically stated, "Not for medical expenses." These special gifts had accumulated into a sizeable sum.

"You've got a few thousand dollars," answered Steve. He wouldn't remind Mitch of the cruise for which some of the money was intended.

"So can I have it?" Mitch asked, matter-of-factly.

"It's yours Mitch. It's money that was given only to you."

"Does that mean I can have it?"

Steve shrugged, "What do you have in mind?"

"It's Christmas, Dad. Kids here need help. I want to give them money." A grin of pure delight lit his face.

Mitchell soon returned to his home, but days later learned that his blood counts had dropped. He needed a blood transfusion. Before Steve loaded him into the car for the trip to the hospital he had gone to the bank. He was ready.

As they pulled out of the drive he said, "Look, Mitchie," and handed Mitchell a stack of money and some envelopes. Now Mitch was ready. Steve could tell by the smile on his face.

Settled into his room, the nurses finished their procedures on Mitch and gave the okay for him to leave. Father and son set off down the hall. Christmas had arrived on 5B.

Mitchell stuffed money into the envelopes as Steve pushed him in his wheelchair. Mitchell knew the rooms he wanted to visit, those families that, even he knew, needed help. And there were others, Steve confided to his gift-bearing son, families whose extreme needs were masked, but which became known to him through discrete inquiries over time.

Anonymity was important. Fortunately most patients' doors were closed, with one very sick kid and a relative inside. After Mitch wrote kid's names on envelopes and filled them with money, Steve slid them under the closed doors.

At the door of one child, whose family was very needy, Mitchell paused, looked at his dad and grinned. Then, reopening the envelope, he added more crisp bills and handed it to Steve, who quietly slid it under the closed door.

As they rolled down the hall, the door opened and a young mother, tears streaming down her cheeks, ran after them waving the envelope they had just deposited. "Is this from you?" she asked gratefully as she approached. Steve offered a slight smile, shrugged his shoulders and pushed off down the hall, without looking back. They'd been found out. Steve hoped the young mother would keep their secret.

"That was really cool, Dad," Mitchell declared as Steve loaded him back into the family van. It was, Steve agreed, really cool.

"Can we do it again, next year?" Mitchell asked, all smiles.

"Yes, son." said Steve as he struggled with painful emotions.

"Dad, I won't be here, will I? I'll be dead." Mitchell's statement was matter-of-fact.

"Yes, son. Unless our miracle happens."

"Then, Dad, you do it. These families need help. Promise!"

"I promise," agreed Steve.

"Pinkie-swear, Dad."

"Pinkie-swear," agreed Steve extending his pinkie

finger to Mitch, who hooked it with his pinkie finger and grinned. There really is a Santa—today it was Mitch.

During Mitchell's brief but painful illness, God blessed the Chepokas family by surrounding them with caring friends who gave of their time and their money. While the miracle of Mitchell's healing was not realized, the miracle of God's provision through the compassion of these friends and strangers alike was very real. Without it, they would not have survived.

By the time Mitchell died, on April 11, 2003, Steve and Becky had formulated the means by which they would implement Steve and Mitchell's pinkie-swear commitment to help the families of critically-ill children.

Just as the purpose of this book is to comfort others through sharing the lessons Mitchell's family learned during their own grieving, the Chepokas' would establish a foundation to provide comfort, and emotional and financial aid to families of critically-ill children, just as they had received. Through this foundation they could be a conduit for God's miraculous provision to other families whose need and burden is similar to what theirs had been.

The balloons released at Mitchell's funeral had barely landed when plans were underway to establish the Miracles of Mitch Foundation. Immediately, Steve established a Board of Directors consisting of local business leaders, church leaders, family and friends whose talents would ensure a strong nucleus. Plans were made to get the work of the foundation underway. What began as an expression of Mitchell's love and concern for children with critical illnesses became a miraculous reality.

On September 29, 2003, less than six months after Mitchell's death, the Foundation established in his name produced its first fund raiser. The golf outing, named the Miracle Open, was a huge success, despite cold winds and occasional sleet, netting a tidy sum for the cause Mitchell intended—financial aid to the families of critically-ill children. The event's guest speaker, whose three-year-old son, AJ, had died of cancer only days earlier, became the fund's first recipient.

Mitchell's burdened heart gave birth to a vision. That vision has become a reality. That reality is only the beginning of the miracles made possible because Mitchell Chepokas lived...and died.

YOU CAN HELP

Proceeds from the purchase of this book will help improve the quality of life for critically-ill children and their families. Portions of every dollar received will go to the *Miracles of Mitch Foundation* to provide financial, emotional and spiritual support for these families.

If you have found this book to be of help to you, we invite you to contact the publishers, AMBER WOODS PUBLISHING, or the *Miracles of Mitch Foundation* and share your story of how Mitchell's life has touched your life or the life of a friend or loved one.

Individuals interested in learning more about the work of the Miracles of Mitch Foundation are encouraged to log onto their website:

www.miraclesofmitchfoundation.org

"Good-bye, Mitch" is available for churches, book clubs, businesses, and organizations at discounted pricing, when purchased in case lots. Please contact the publisher or the Foundation for specific pricing information. Volume discounts will reduce available foundation funds.

"Mitchell, Mommy misses you, buddy!!!"

"Jesus, please give my Mitchie boy a big hug for me! Thanx!"

Becky